WHAT'S A
SEQUENCER?

A Basic Guide to Their Features and Use

by Greg R. Starr

revised by Emile Menasché

HAL•LEONARD®
CORPORATION

7777 W. BLUEMOUND RD. P.O. BOX 13819 MILWAUKEE, WI 53213

ISBN 0-634-01345-9

HAL•LEONARD®
CORPORATION
7777 W. BLUEMOUND RD. P.O. BOX 13819 MILWAUKEE, WI 53213

Visit Hal Leonard Online at
www.halleonard.com

CONTENTS

INTRODUCTION

*Do I need a degree in computer science to operate
a sequencer, and if so, what's wrong with playing
my old penny whistle anyway?*

ASKED YOURSELF THIS QUESTION LATELY? Does it seem as
if the march of technology is giving you blisters? Not even sure
if you want to get your boots on? Well, tie up those laces. Using
the latest music technology isn't magic and doesn't require a
Ph.D. in electrical engineering or rocket science. A little patience,
a smidgen of knowledge, and some hands-on experience are all
you need to get the most out of your sequencer, whether you
have a basic sequencer built into your portable keyboard or a
full-blown digital audio/MIDI program loaded into your personal computer.

A sequencer will open new horizons in your musical creativity,
making it possible for you to play with a band that you create,
to capture and alter your performances, and to write out your
music with greater ease than ever before. The sequencer is a key
component in the modern recording studio.

Many Names, Work the Same

Sequencers come in variety of forms and are known by many
names. But whether they are called "Performance Recorders,"

1

"Music Production Software," "MIDI Sequence Recorders," or simply "Sequencers," they all perform roughly the same function. Their sole purpose is the storage of incoming data (information) for playback through a compatible instrument. Wow, does that sound like a lot! For now, think of a sequencer as a fancy electronic tape recorder that will record the notes you play into it.

Many of today's sequencers include both MIDI and digital audio functions. (Chapter 3 explains MIDI, Chapter 6 introduces digital audio). Consequently, much of this book is devoted to using such units with electronic keyboards and other MIDI-compatible equipment. It's worth noting, however, that some sequencers built into portable or home keyboards don't "speak MIDI."

If you own a sequencer, this book will cover both the basics of using it and the more advanced "goodies" that are available on some models. If you don't have a sequencer and are thinking of buying one (or a keyboard with one built in), you'll find enough information here to ask the right questions and decide which model is right for your particular needs.

So please come in, take your shoes off. We'll get you some moleskin for those blisters. Check your penny whistle at the door.

1.

SO, WHAT IS A SEQUENCER?

PEOPLE HAVE ALWAYS BEEN FASCINATED by machines that play music. Music boxes and player pianos have held an attraction for most people. Just take a peek into a music box shop at a local shopping mall. People stand and marvel at these wonderful little devices that plunk out their favorite songs. They will stand for long periods of time and smile when they finally remember the name of the tune they are listening to. (Children often play for hours with a simpler version of the same thing: the jack-in-the-box.)

A familiar mechanical sequencer

These incredible contraptions are really mechanical sequencers. Someone has programmed the music by sticking pins into a drum or disk. The notes are played back at a rate determined by the speed of the disk or drum. Speed up the music box, the music gets faster. Slow it down and the music gets slower. Notice, though, that in both speeding up and slowing down the mechanism, the pitch of the notes doesn't change. Slowing a music box down isn't the same as slowing a tape down, where the speed of the tape determines the pitch. This distinction will be important to the discussion of sequencers in the following chapters.

Just like a music box, a player piano is a type of mechanical sequencer. A pianist plays the piano while a roll of paper runs through a mechanism that punches a series of holes in it. During playback, the piano "reads" these holes and plays the appropriate notes. And just like the music box, speeding up the piano roll doesn't change the pitch of any note that is played. It only changes the speed at which the notes are played back.

What It Is, What It Does

The term "sequencer" has its origin in the days of analog synthesizers, when the electonic signals that generated sound could be recorded and stored for playback. Today, with the proliferation of recording and editing tools and the intermingling of technologies, the better question might be, "What does a sequencer do?"

A sequencer is an arranging tool. It allows you to record and edit a piece of music. Along the way, you can change aspects of the performance (like the timing and pitch of notes) and many aspects of the production (the character and sound of those notes). The capabilities of a sequencer can vary widely — from the relative simplicity of a keyboard's built-in sequencer to the pro-level production power available from a high-end computer package. The principles that govern how a sequencer works are largely rooted in the same idea: looking at music as a series of events that occur over time.

These events can be:

- MIDI notes
- Audio recordings
- Performance Controller Data (such as pitch bend, after-touch, etc.)
- Mix Controller Data (volume, pan)
- Program changes
- System Exclusive data
- Tempo changes and more

Sequencers come in many forms: the dedicated drum machine; the stand alone MIDI sequencer (and its modern offshoot, the multi-track "beat box"), the arpeggiator, the built-in arranger found on a home keyboard, the more elaborate built-in sequencer found on keyboard workstations, and the computer-based software sequencer/audio recorder.

Not all sequencers can work with all of these event types, and not all work with them in the same way, but all let you manipulate these events in some way *after they have been recorded*. You can change a note's pitch, re-map its pitch bend, change the timing, loop a specific section, erase notes that you don't want to hear, and much, much more. None of these tools are available in a traditional linear tape recorder.

But what will it do for you? Why use a sequencer instead of a traditional tape recorder? Well, what if you had the sounds of an entire band at your fingertips and could record each part separately, then play them all back simultaneously while you played along? Or what if you were writing a piece of music and decided that instead of piano, you'd like to hear it with strings? Or what if you are all fumble-fingered but have some great musical ideas that you want to hear? All of these things are possible with a sequencer. Through the use of a sequencer, you can experience the joy that making music is supposed to be.

2.

HERE'S THE BASICS

TODAY'S SEQUENCERS ARE ELECTRONIC, rather than mechanical, in nature and they come in a variety of forms. Some are dedicated hardware units — boxes whose sole purpose in life is to record and play back musical information. Others are built into electronic keyboards — augmenting the list of sounds and other capabilities that such instruments possess. Still others don't exist as physical objects at all, but instead are programs that are run on personal computers.

No matter what form they come in, sequencers all perform the same function. They all record what is played into them and then play it back for you. This in itself isn't particularly earth-shattering. An ordinary tape recorder can do the same thing. So what makes a sequencer so special?

A Magic Recorder

A sequencer is most easily thought of as a "magic" tape recorder. Most of the controls are the same ones found on a tape deck. Play, Record, Stop, Pause — these are controls you probably are familiar with. They do the same job, whether on a sequencer or a cassette player. If you want to play a sequence, press Play. If you want to record into the sequencer, press Record. The basic operation of the machine is the same, whether tape deck or sequencer. But unlike a tape recorder, a sequencer records data that can be manipulated after the fact. What you play into a sequencer is only the beginning of the creative process.

Welcome to the Grid

To understand how a sequencer works, you must first understand that every sequencer — from the simplest beatbox to the flashiest software package — looks at your music as a grid. This grid is like a graph that tracks events which happen over time, placing each event into a slot on the graph.

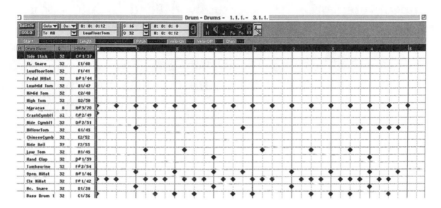

A visual representation of the grid

In the early sequencers, these slots were of relatively low resolution, which meant that the slots on the grid were pretty far apart. For example, on a grid with a resolution of a quarter note, the sequencer would only be able to play back quarter notes. If a group of sixteenth notes were played into it, these notes would be moved (or quantized) to the nearest quarter note.

A quarter-note grid has limited musical value, but early sequencers and drum machines with resolutions of a sixteenth note *were* popular (some remain in wide use today). However, they were somewhat mechanical sounding, taking away the subtleties that are characteristic of a human performance.

Modern sequencers still use a grid, but that grid is made up of much smaller chunks of time: Instead of being limited to sixteenth notes (4 parts per quarter note, or **ppq**) modern sequencers can have resolutions in the hundreds, and in some cases, thousands of ppq. The higher the resolution, the more accurately the sequencer reproduces what you play into it — the more natural the performance will feel. Of course, you can still restrict the resolution of the grid if you want by adjusting the sequencer's quantization settings.

It's important to get used to the mathematical way a sequencer views your music. A sequencer usually divides the grid as follows: Bar:Beat:Sub-beat or clock (usually defined by the ppq). For example, if the display shows a note at 3:2:240 (and your sequencer has a resolution of 480 ppq), you're looking at the eighth-note following the second beat in bar (or measure) three. (The 240 represents half the number of ticks that make up a quarter note.)

Tempo Tempo

In order for the grid to have any meaning, you must first define a tempo for the piece you're recording. All sequencers let you assign a metronome or "click track" to play along with and keep you in time.

Once recorded, sequencers let you play back the recorded data at a tempo different than the original without changing the pitch of the song. The note data aren't changed, just played faster or slower. This can be pretty handy for those of us who aren't virtuosic on the keyboard. A difficult piece or section of music can be recorded at a slow tempo, then played back at a faster one.

Sounds Like . . . Just About Anything!

Imagine taking a piano roll off of a player piano and putting it on a player organ instead. Or a player harpsichord. Because the performance information recorded on the roll isn't the actual sound of the performance, that information can be played back on a different instrument than was used for recording.

The situation is similar with electronic sequencers. You can play back the same notes on a different instrument, or a different sound on the same instrument. If you don't like the piano part in a piece, you can hear it with strings instead. Try that with a tape recorder!

Cut/Copy/Paste

Most sequencers let you copy and paste data from one region of a sequence to another. If you are recording a section of music that will repeat 67 times, there is no point in going through the drudgery of playing that section 67 times. Copy the repeated section and paste it in the appropriate places.

Because of the advance of technology, the distinction between different types of sequencers keeps changing. These days, there are hardware sequencers that offer much of the power previously reserved for computer-based packages; conversely, many computer packages now offer the "stand-alone" simplicity once only found in the hardware domain. For the sake of our discussion, we'll look at two basic types:

- Hardware sequencers, which come as independent "stand-alone units," or as part of a keyboard workstation

- Software sequencers that run on a personal computer

But before getting into the specifics of the various options out there, we'll look at the language sequencers use to communicate with the world at large: MIDI.

3.

THE ROAD TO MIDI

WHAT IS MIDI, AND WHY SHOULD YOU CARE? Before answering this question, let's take a few steps back and peer into the dark regions of history before MIDI came into being.

Early Sequencers

Sherman, set the Wayback machine for the early days of synthesizers (early 1970s). These early **analog** synths were controlled by variations in voltage. (Suffice it to say that the higher the voltage that went into the sound generator, the higher the pitch that was generated.) An analog sequencer, as part of this control-voltage system, would spit out preprogrammed voltages to the sound generator to produce a series of notes. These sequencers could typically produce only 16 different notes, and each note had to be tuned individually by turning a knob or moving a slider. These modules, though advanced for the time, quickly developed a reputation for sounding dull and mechanical. Incessantly repeating patterns played over and over became less novel and started sounding boring and dated. Just over the horizon, however, were the first **digital** sequencers.

Dig it All

The first digital sequencers were a blend of the then-new digital (computer) technology and the old analog (voltage) technology. They combined digital memory with control-voltage outputs to create a digital/analog hybrid. These new units solved two of the biggest limitations of the old analog modules, namely the number of notes and tuning. They had digital memory, which expanded the note capacity to 250 to 1,000 notes (depending on the model). They could also be calibrated so the output voltages that drove the sound generators were very accurate. (The old analog units were notoriously inaccurate and hence notoriously out of tune.)

On the earliest of these sequencers, as on their analog predecessors, you had to specify the pitch of each note one at a time — a procedure known as **step-time input**. Later models allowed you to actually sit down at the keyboard and play (imagine!) while the sequencer recorded — something called **real-time input**. But even this new blend of technologies had its shortcomings.

Imagine yourself recording into a sequencer. You have been trying to record a piano part for the past two hours. You are just playing the last flawless phrase when Fido, the faithful family dog, decides that he wants to show his undying affection by giving you doggy kisses. Of course, this interruption causes you excessive anguish because in the process of receiving these enthusiastic doggy kisses, you make a blatant mistake in the part you were recording. With most of the digital/analog hybrid sequencers, editing (changing) a single event such as a wrong note was impossible. The only option after Fido's emotional outburst was to rerecord the entire part from the beginning.

Not only was editing a problem, but compatibility was also an issue. Brand X's sequencer might or might not work with Brand Y's synthesizer (most likely not). Only certain sequencers would work with certain keyboards, usually from the same manufacturer. These systems, although powerful for the time, were doomed to extinction when the MIDI specification was developed in the early 1980s.

And Then Along Came MIDI

In 1982, a common language — MIDI — was adopted by manufacturers of keyboards and synthesizers. MIDI (Musical Instrument Digital Interface) is a language that keyboards and other compatible equipment speak to each other, allowing them to communicate.

So what's the big deal? Imagine you are at the United Nations. A monumental decision has been made that all communication at the UN will now be made in a common language. No matter where you are from, you can communicate with anyone that is at the UN in this common language. Well, that is what MIDI did for synthesizers and keyboards. No matter what manufacturer made the keyboard, it can communicate with any other MIDI-compatible keyboard or device (like a sequencer!). No longer is a user limited to any one manufacturer or system. You now can mix and match equipment to suit your particular needs.

MIDI is arguably the most important advance in music since the invention of music notation. It is impossible (very difficult, at least) to escape, and it has made music making both more powerful and more enjoyable for the general public.

If an instrument doesn't speak MIDI, you won't be able to play it from a MIDI sequencer. A non-MIDI instrument won't under-stand what the sequencer is trying to tell it. It also won't have a MIDI port (a fancy word for a connection) on the back.

IN   OUT   THRU

MIDI ports

4.
COMMON FEATURES

SEQUENCERS COME IN A VARIETY of shapes, sizes, colors, and prices. Some look like the control panel of a jet fighter, while others have only a few tiny buttons on a deceptively simple looking front panel. They vary greatly in features and how you interact with them, but there are a number of basic features common to all.

In the Channel, On the Track

Before we look more closely at features, we need to clarify a couple of terms. When the word **channel** is used, it is implied that a MIDI channel is being discussed. When the word **track** is used, it is a recording/playback track on a sequencer. Why should you know the difference? What is the difference, anyway?

Let's say, for example, that you're recording a piano piece into a 16-track sequencer, and your piano sound is assigned to MIDI channel 1 on your system. You might want to use all 16 tracks, recording a new take to each before deciding which one you like best. All 16 tracks would be used up, but only one MIDI channel would be used. After deciding which parts you like best, you could compile them into one track, freeing up the others to record additional instruments.

Many multitrack sequencers allow you to put multiple MIDI channels on each track. There are also sequencers that allow only a single MIDI channel on a single track.

Some sequencers allow you to direct each track to more than one MIDI channel on playback. For example, if you've recorded a part on track 1, you might play it back on MIDI channels 4 and 7 to direct it to two different instruments; but both instruments would play the same notes.

Getting In and Out

Think of your sequencer as a clearinghouse of musical information. Once connected to an interface, a sequencer will allow you to input MIDI data using a controller such as a keyboard and route that data in real time to any other device in your system (including back to the original controller). The device that generates the sound is determined by the "thru" setting or the instrument assigned to the current record track. Many computer sequencers also allow you to route MIDI to more than one port or channel at a time, allowing you to build layered sounds consisting of several instruments playing the same part.

Remember, MIDI is a communications interface — it tells your equipment what to do. The problem with a complicated MIDI system is that when something isn't doing what it's supposed to, the reason for the problem is not always obvious. Fortunately, your MIDI equipment should have some visual monitoring capabilities that tell you whether the computer or interface is receiving MIDI.

Making Tracks

Once MIDI information is flowing the way you need it to, recording is extremely easy: Simply arm a track, start the sequencer, and start playing. With most software packages, you have the option of dealing with your performance in pattern or linear fashion. You can record MIDI data destructively or non-destructively, keep as many versions of the same track as you want, record while looping the same few bars over and over, and much more. And you can automate and preprocess MIDI data (for example, setting values for transposition and harmonization).

So far, we've talked a lot about sequencers recording data. But what type of data is it? What kind of information gets recorded into a sequencer track in the first place? Well, first of all, notes are recorded, along with a "time stamp" that tells the sequencer when to play a particular note. But what else? Music is more than just a string of notes played at the right time. There must be more in a track than just that. Well, there is. Here are other kinds of data that a sequencer will record:

- **Note Length.** The sequencer will record how long each key is held down. A note will continue to sound for that length of time. When a key is pressed, the keyboard sends a message to the sequencer saying, "This key is down now." When you release the key, the keyboard will send a message to the sequencer saying, "This key is up now." Upon playback, the sequencer will tell the keyboard or sound module to play and "hold down" that note until it tells the keyboard to release the note.

- **Key Velocity.** This is the force at which a key gets pressed. Usually, the faster (or harder) a key is played, the louder the note sounds.

- **Pitch Bend.** If your keyboard has a pitch bend wheel or lever, your sequencer may be able to record its movement. Pitch bends on such instruments as flute or sax can be very effective. Your sequencer may allow you to edit that pitch bend as well, if you didn't get it quite right the first time.

- **Controller Data.** This category is a bit of a catch-all. Controller data can be a number of different things. When you press the sustain pedal, for example, the keyboard sends out a controller message. This message is recorded by the sequencer. Upon playback, the sequencer transmits this controller message back to the instrument along with the note data, triggering the sustain function.

The modulation wheel ("mod wheel" for short) is another common controller. Modulation is often used to add vibrato to notes. There other controllers as well — including volume, pan, and aftertouch — but these two are the most common.

- **Patch Change.** Within a single track, it is possible to program the sequencer to change sounds for you. Instead of reaching over to the instrument and changing sounds (commonly called Patches) by hand, you can have the sequencer do it for you. Using patch changes, it is possible to change the sound of a track in mid-stream.

First Edition

Sequencers allow you to edit (change) the data within a track. By editing the tracks of a sequence, you can correct any mistakes you might have made while recording. Is Fido still at your feet, waiting to show his undying affection? Made one tiny mistake in an otherwise flawless and truly inspired performance? No problem! You can correct that mistake from the sequencer and perfect the performance. The extent of these editing features will vary from one model of sequencer to the next. Some will allow you to edit nearly any element of a track (and there are a lot of them!) while others will only provide minimal editing facilities.

Bells and Whistles

Sequencers also come with a number of bells and whistles that make the recording process more precise. (Not literal bells or whistles. That's just a figure of speech.) These include *quantization, transposition and harmonization, velocity scaling, step-time input, punch-in recording, track shifting,* and *looping.*

Quantization is a fancy word for a process that will correct small rhythmic errors in your playing. Quantizing to a certain value will line up notes in the track to the nearest multiple of that note value. For example, if you quantize a track to 16th notes, all notes in that track will line up exactly on the nearest 16th note. This can be a handy feature to have if your playing needs occasional help. Many sequencers let you decide how much quantization is applied to a passage of notes. For a tighter performance that retains a natural feel, you can set your sequencer up to adjust notes by a specified percentage, or use the "range" command to quantize only the notes that are close to the grid value, leaving others alone.

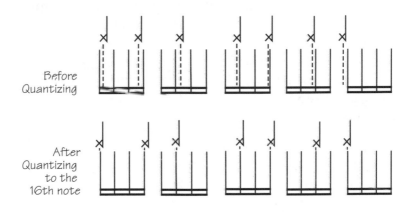

Before Quantizing

After Quantizing to the 16th note

Swing and **Groove** are other related quantize functions. Swing determines the position of some note values. For example, if you set up an eighth note quantize with 50 percent swing, all the eighth notes will be evenly spaced. Change the swing to 75 percent, and the upbeats will be moved later, as in a jazz swing arrangement.

Groove quantize is a complex combination of all the above parameters. Groove templates are usually derived from an outside source, such as the playing of a real drummer. Instead of restricting every note in a passage to a specific value, grooves often move different notes to different grid positions, mimicking the variations of a real performance. Many grooves change the velocity of a part, as well as the timing. They are especially effective on drum tracks.

All multitrack sequencers allow you to apply different quantization values to be applied to specific tracks (or parts of tracks). Many sequencers also allow you to set a "playback-only" quantize that doesn't change the original note data. If you're sure you want to restrict your playing to a specified grid, your sequencer may allow you to set "input quantize," which corrects the timing of the notes as they are played.

In addition to letting you massage timing without altering pitch, almost all sequencers let you **transpose** and **harmonize** the pitch of the notes after you've recorded them without changing the timing. You can select individual notes or groups of notes and move them chromatically (in half steps). This is useful if you have to take an arrangement down a half-step to accommodate a singer or double a bass part with a piano an octave higher.

Some sequencers also let you predefine a key, scale, and interval, instead of a chromatic value. This way, you can shift a part by thirds and have the note remain in the correct key.

Instead of shifting the original passage, the harmonize function creates new notes that harmonize with the parts you've played in. Like the transpose function, these harmonies can be chromatic or they can follow a specific key and scale.

Most electronic instruments track dynamic changes by **velocity** — the speed at which you hit a key. Most sequencers let you adjust the velocity of an original performance to suit your needs. There are usually several choices: edit single notes, edit entire tracks (or sections of a track), or edit notes specified by some criteria. Velocity editing can be used to create crescendos; add life to a drum groove; or even, depending on the capabilities of your synths, to switch between voices in a layered sound.

Step-time input (or step entry) is useful when you are trying to record a particularly difficult section. It allows you to enter notes one at a time, while the sequencer waits patiently after each note for you to enter the next one. It is an alternative to real-time recording (normal recording-as-you-play). With step-time recording, you can enter music that is too complex for real-time entry, or that is too difficult for you to play technically.

If this step-time business sounds familiar, it's because it is a throwback to the early sequencers mentioned in Chapter 3. It just goes to show that sometimes the best ideas are old ones.

What happens when you have entered a part but want to re-record a single measure somewhere in the middle of the song? Enter **punch-in recording**. This feature will turn the Record button on and off automatically at points you specify. No more reaching over to try and hit the Stop button before you record over parts you want to keep. You can tell the sequencer when to "press" Record and when to turn it off.

Track shifting allows you to move a track forward or backward in time, relative to the other tracks. You can generally move the track by measures, beats, clocks (the parts per quarter note discussed earlier), or any combination of the three. Moving by clocks is often important in establishing the proper "feel" for a track. For example, if you decide that your piano part sounds better as a mellow string part, you may need to shift the track ahead to compensate for the slow attack of the strings, so they don't sound "behind the beat." The greater the timing resolution of the sequencer, the more precise you can be in shifting a track.

In the Loop

A sequencer's **loop** feature is one of its biggest advantages over a traditional linear recorder. Loops can be used in different ways in recording and arranging a piece of music.

Loop recording is really useful when you're starting a new song. Many sequencers allow you to repeat a section of the song over and over (you define the section) and play along as it repeats. Many sequencers give you a choice: you can have each pass add to the current track, replace the current track, or create a new track. (Some even automatically mute the old takes!) When you're ready to go to the next part of the song, simply re-define the loop and repeat the process.

Looping can also be used to repeat a specified section of a track or group of tracks. You can specify the beginning and end points of the loop and the number of times you wish the loop to play. If you want to play back the drum part of a song's chorus twice, for instance, set the loop and let the sequencer do the work. This can speed the arranging process and cut down the number of notes you play in when recording a track.

The term loop is also applied to pre-recorded snippets of audio — such as drum parts — that can be played back by a sampler or, in the case of many software packages, by the sequencer itself.

Patterns 'n' More

A feature similar to looping is **pattern-based recording**. Some sequencers, and almost all drum machines, use this approach. A pattern, usually one to four measures in length, is repeated by the machine. As in the loop example above, you add new parts on the fly as you build the pattern layer by layer. In a drum machine, for instance, record the bass drum the first time through the pattern. Then add the snare drum as the machine repeats the pattern. Keep adding things until you have finished the pattern. Then go on to record the remaining patterns and link them together to form a song.

A related approach found in some sequencers allows you to record individual **sequences** which can then be assembled into **songs**. For example, a pop ballad might consist of five sequences: an intro, a verse, a chorus, a bridge, and an ending. Each of these would only have to be recorded once. But when assembled into a song, they could be played back in any order, any number of times. For example: intro, verse, verse, chorus, verse, chorus, bridge, chorus, chorus, ending, as illustrated on the following page.

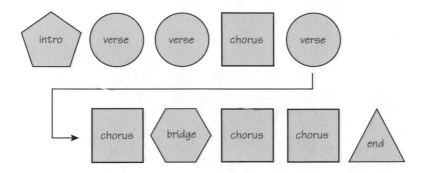

Slipped Disk

Once you have recorded and polished a sequence, you probably will want to store it somehow. Although some sequencers still rely on internal memory or ROM cards for storage, most offer a floppy or removable **disk drive** that lets you save and load sequences quickly and easily. Others have no internal means of storage; these can often "dump" their memory into an external sequencer or software package via MIDI System Exclusive Messages (Sysex).

These are just a few of the features that may be on a particular model of sequencer. When shopping, don't be afraid to ask questions about the features of a particular unit. Read the manual and advertising literature to see if a specific sequencer will be right for you.

5.
HARDWARE
SEQUENCERS

HARDWARE SEQUENCER DOES NOT REFER to a method of organizing the tools in your garage, and it doesn't refer to a recorder that uses mechanical parts to store information. A hardware, or stand-alone, sequencer is a unit that is self-contained and works with its own proprietary recording software.

Stand-alone sequencers can range from elaborate production stations that rival software packages in power (and price), to miniature units small enough to fit in a shirt pocket.

These products offer some advantages over software sequencers (which are discussed in Chapter 6): They're self-contained, so you don't have to lug a computer or external interface to use them; the hardware is designed to work with the software, so they rarely crash; some even offer knobs or other interactive programming and performance tools.

Many musicians also feel that hardware sequencers offer better timing than their computer-based counterparts because there is less "software overhead" to interfere with the music.

There are disadvantages, too: While the top models offer large displays, even these can't rival those found on a typical computer screen. Memory is more limited in a hardware sequencer, as is track capacity. A hardware sequencer will typically be able to address 16 to 32 MIDI channels; depending on the interface, a computer-based system can address hundreds of separate MIDI channels.

Shapes and Sizes

The most basic form of hardware sequencer is the **drum machine.** It can record and store rhythm patterns and play them back using its own internal sounds or, through MIDI, the sounds of other instruments. A number of patterns can be strung together to form a complete song.

A basic drum machine can record on only one channel and most of them lack storage facilities such as disk drives. Most can, however, transmit and receive MIDI notes, lock with other sequencers via MIDI, and dump their memory into a storage program via Sysex. Some drum machines offer bass sounds in addition to a wide variety of drum samples.

Arpeggiators create real-time patterns of notes based on a pre-defined scale. Although stand-alone arpeggiators are rare these days, arpeggiation is a feature found on many synths and as a component to many sequencers. With an arpeggiator, you're not playing the scale itself — you simply hold one or two notes; the arpeggiator does the rest. Most sequencers that offer arpeggiation let you synch the pattern to the tempo of the song and permanently store the pattern as MIDI notes.

More elaborate **stand-alone sequencers** come in a wide variety of styles, sizes, and price points, from the battery-powered pocket models to the full-featured table-top variety to groove boxes — units that combine the multi track features of a sequencer with the sounds and interface of a drum machine or synthesizer.

Typically, even the smallest stand-alone sequencer offers a battery of internal sounds, can trigger sounds in other MIDI devices, and can synch to external devices via MIDI clocks or MIDI Time Code. The memory capacity of these units usually ranges from 10,000 to hundreds of thousands of notes. Stand-alone sequencers often offer a combination of **linear** and **pattern-based** recording. Patterns (explained in Chapter 4) are good for creating drum and bass parts, while linear tracks are generally the way to go for lead instruments.

Since they make good musical sketch-pads, many stand-alone sequencers offer built-in arranging functions to help you get started in composing a new song. Some of the beefier models offer expandable RAM memory, SCSI ports for attaching external storage devices, sampling capability, clock resolutions up to 480 ppq (pulses per quarter note), and extensive MIDI control features. Some can even record linear audio tracks onto an internal hard drive.

(Work)stations Everybody

For many music hobbyists (as well as a number of professional players), home and portable keyboards are the ideal do-it-all instruments. With their variety of instrumental sounds, drum rhythms, and easy-to-play automatic accompaniment, they are the contemporary answer to the one-man bands of yesteryear. When you add a sequencer to this equation, the result can be a pretty enticing instrument. There are two kinds:

- Those that record only on a single part, or track. Depending on the model of keyboard you have, you can separately record automatic accompaniment (easy-play chords and automatic rhythm) or melody notes into this track. Or you may be able to record both automatic accompaniment and a melody line into this single track at the same time.

- Those that have multiple tracks for you to record on. Again, depending on the model of your keyboard, the types of information recorded onto a track will vary. It may be only automatic accompaniment, only melody notes, or both at the same time. Some home keyboards have sequencers that rival those found on professional workstations.

Professional **keyboard workstations** are an extension of this self-accompaniment concept. While most don't offer the built-in arrangement tools found on home keyboards, they make up for it by being more flexible and easier to integrate into a complete

MIDI system, offering up to 32 record tracks, multiple MIDI outs, extensive synch functions, and more. Some of the sequencers found on these devices are basic "sketch-pads." Others offer recording power to rival top-end sequencers, with up to 480 ppq resolution, internal hard disk recording capabilities, extensive editing functionality, and more.

One of the big advantages of a full-featured workstation is that it gives you the best of both worlds. It communicates internally without MIDI, so finding the right sound for each track — and making sure that sound loads correctly every time you want to play the song back — is much easier on a workstation than on a complex MIDI rig. But it can also use MIDI to communicate with other devices in your system.

Setting Standards

Many hardware (and software) sequencers — both stand-alone and those found in home and professional keyboards — can play back **Standard MIDI Files (SMFs)**. SMFs are sequences that follow a standard specification as to sound and controller assignments. This lets them play back correctly on the wide variety of compatible instruments that follow the **General MIDI (GM)** standard. SMFs can be read and played across almost all platforms that address MIDI, so an SMF created on one person's computer can be loaded and played back on someone else's stand-alone sequencer — great if you want to take your home-recorded tunes on the road or share files with colleagues. There are even devices that specialize in the playback of SMFs but offer no recording and editing capabilities of their own.

6.

SOFTWARE
SOLUTIONS

IF YOU ALREADY OWN A PERSONAL COMPUTER, a software sequencer may be the best option for your sequencing needs. It may save you money and provide you with a more powerful system, albeit a less portable one, than a hardware device. Sequencing software is available for all common personal computers, ranging in features from the very powerful to the very, very, very powerful.

A decade ago, computer sequencers were just beginning to come into their own as viable recording tools. Back in the day, memory was at a premium and storage, by today's standards, was nonexistent. (Those of you who remember working with 640k of RAM and feeling flush at the idea of having a 20MB hard disk at your disposal know what I mean.) Back then, a long song full of MIDI data could use up all of a computer's resources.

Times sure have changed. Computers have become faster, RAM has become more plentiful, and hard drives of 20 gigabytes, which offer 1,000 times the storage of those old disks, have become commonplace. (I'm sure that they'll be considered small by the time many of you read this.) Thanks to these technological leaps, computers can not only record almost unlimited amounts of MIDI data, they can handle multi-track digital audio, process that audio in real time, and even connect internally to software-based synthesizers and samplers, reducing the need for any external hardware.

Advantages and Disadvantages

Remember how we said that sequencers treat music as data? Computers are excellent tools for viewing, cataloguing, and manipulating data. The relatively large display alone is a strong argument for using a computer.

A computer is also open-ended: A piece of software should be able to address a wide variety of hardware and be easily reconfigured to handle the task at hand, whatever it may be. Also, these days, almost all computer-based sequencers combine MIDI and audio recording into one powerful system. This allows you to record MIDI backing tracks alongside live vocals, work with pre recorded drum loops and bass patterns, and, as we'll see later in this chapter, much more.

Computers also present some disadvantages, however. Desktop and tower machines are bulky, can be noisy, and are often expected to perform non-musical duties — word processing comes to mind — that don't always mix well with making music.

Computers can also be temperamental when it comes to dealing with music data. Many people feel that the time it takes a computer to address an interface and transmit MIDI data through that interface has a negative impact on the music's timing. An overworked computer can crash in mid-session, a far less likely occurrence when dealing with a dedicated hardware unit.

Still, for many musicians, these are small considerations compared to the absolute power and flexibility afforded by a computer-based system.

What You Need

Although many computers offer some internal MIDI capability, let's assume that you want your computer sequencer to address external MIDI and audio devices. Assuming you already have a computer, you'll need:

- Software
- A MIDI interface
- MIDI controllers and a sound source
- An audio card (optional)
- Audio monitoring system
- All the appropriate MIDI and audio cables to connect your system (see the next chapter.)

The Grid: Computer-Style

Remember, every sequencer looks at music in terms of a grid: a series of events that occur over a period of time. Although many software packages support event-list and notation-type editing, the majority use the grid model as the central display of both MIDI and audio data.

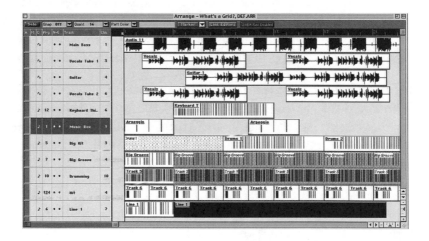

A typical computer sequencer displays music in grid form.

Most of the action occurs in an overview window, which shows all the tracks in the current song or sequence. (Note: this window has different names depending on the software package: Tracks and Arrange are the two most popular.)

A timeline goes across the top of the window, displaying the location of the song in bars and beats, or in some cases, in minutes and seconds. The contents of each track is displayed underneath the time line. Many packages allow you to see a depiction of the actual audio and MIDI events within each track. In most cases, a track can be subdivided into segments (again, different packages call these subdivisions by different names), and these segments can be named, copied, moved, and edited in a wide variety of ways.

Other information you'll see in the typical overview includes:

- Track name and instrument assignment
- Current patch
- Mute and Solo status
- Any nondestructive editing applications, such as quantize, transpose, velocity limit, etc.
- User comments

This visual overview gives you a comprehensive look at what the music is doing. You can see at a glance that a drum roll leading into the guitar solo is a measure too early, or that the horn pad goes on too long. You can also see how the tracks are assigned to the devices in your rig, and determine which tracks are active and which are muted. This can help you figure out why you're hearing a tuba sound instead of the piano you expected.

Most packages allow you to place markers in this overview window (some display the markers in all edit windows), which can be used to set up quick locate points. You can zoom out to look at an entire arrangement at a glance, or zoom in to focus on a specific section you wish to edit.

Going Inside with a View Toward Flexibility

One of the advantages of using a software sequencer is the flexibility in editing MIDI and audio data. The ability to see large amounts of data in a variety of forms can make the sequencer easier to use than a hardware model.

For instance, the data contained in a track can be edited using an **event list**. In an event list, all events, such as note information, pitch bend, audio clippings, and any MIDI controller data, are listed in the order they are performed. Here is a portion of an event list:

List – Track 5 – 1.1.1.– 5.3.3.

Start Position	Length	Val1	Val2	Val3	Event Type	Chn	Comment
1. 1. 1. 0	2.1618	A#2/53	95	54	Note	2	
1. 1. 1. 0	3. 80	C1/35	119	54	Note	2	
1. 1. 1. 0	3.1744	C4/72	38	54	Note	2	
1. 1. 1. 0	1. 232	F#4/73	93	54	Note	2	muted
1. 1. 3. 86	0.2034	F#4/73	53	54	Note	2	
1. 1. 3. 86	0.2898	F#2/54	75	54	Note	2	
1. 1. 4. 743	0.2553	F#4/73	54	54	Note	2	
1. 2. 1. 138	1.2754	G#2/55	75	54	Note	2	
1. 2. 1. 138	0.1705	G#4/83	135	54	Note	2	
1. 2. 1. 160	1. 464	D4/74	95	54	Note	2	
1. 2. 3. 138	0.2102	F#4/73	31	54	Note	2	
1. 2. 3. 138	0.2654	F#2/54	75	54	Note	2	
1. 2. 4.3360	----.----	1	1	---	Modulation	1	
1. 3. 1. 0	----.----	1	2	---	Modulation	1	
1. 3. 1. 51	0.1809	F#4/73	134	54	Note	2	
1. 3. 1. 51	1.2749	A#2/53	79	54	Note	2	
1. 3. 1.2880	----.----	1	3	---	Modulation	1	
1. 3. 2. 584	0.3200	D4/74	56	54	Note	2	
1. 3. 2.1440	----.----	1	4	---	Modulation	1	
1. 3. 2.3048	1. 952	C4/72	38	54	Note	2	
1. 3. 3. 0	----.----	1	5	---	Modulation	1	
1. 3. 3. 0	----.----	10	70	---	Pan	1	
1. 3. 3. 51	1.2748	F#4/73	59	54	Note	2	
1. 3. 3. 51	0.2481	F#2/54	33	54	Note	2	
1. 3. 3.2400	----.----	10	73	---	Pan	1	
1. 3. 3.3360	----.----	1	7	---	Modulation	1	
1. 3. 4. 570	1.1947	G#2/55	55	54	Note	2	

Event list

Another way to view MIDI data is in **graphic notation**. This form provides the best depiction of our famous grid. Each note is displayed as a bar: The length of a note is shown by the length of the bar; the longer the bar, the longer the note. Other information, such as pitch bend and note velocity, is displayed either on the grid with the note information or below it in a separate area of the screen. Here is the same set of notes as seen in graphic notation:

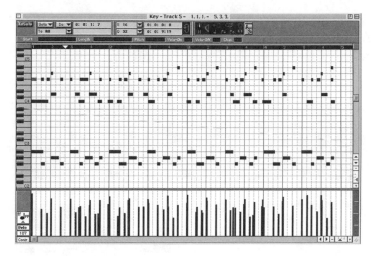

Graphic notation

You can also display controller data in special graphical windows that streamline the editing process.

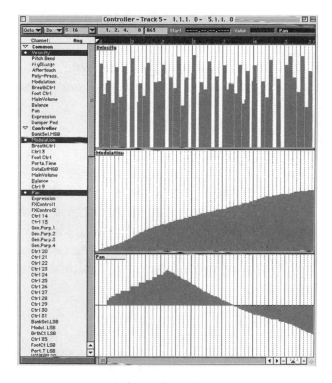

Controller editor

Another feature that can make editing even easier is **notation editing**. Here, MIDI note messages are displayed as notes on a normal musical staff. Other MIDI information is usually displayed below the staff, much like the graphic editing mode.

Here the same notes again, displayed in notation editing:

Many software packages allow you to create complex scores for printout. They can even create custom staves, tablature, and chord symbols.

So What?

All right, so why go through all the trouble of seeing the same thing in three different forms? What's all the commotion about? Well, not only can you view the data in the form of your choice, but you can also view it in the form that will make it the easiest to edit. Each of these views makes certain tasks easier to perform. Different modes have their unique merits as well as their drawbacks.

Event lists are sequential. The events that are listed are displayed in the order they are performed. (MIDI is serial in nature. MIDI commands are sent one at a time, but fast enough that events can sound like they happen at the same time.) This can be handy for things such as pedaling commands. For instance, suppose you want to make sure the last chord in a measure is held with the sustain pedal. An event list will tell you exactly where the pedal command is in relation to the chord. If the pedal command is listed before the note commands for the chord, the pedal command is sent before the note commands are sent. Hence, the notes of the chord will be held by the pedal. By viewing things in the order they occur, you can make sure that events happen in the order you want them to.

Graphic editing makes viewing the lengths of notes easy, as well as viewing controller events such as pitch bend. For instance, if a single note in a chord is playing longer than it should, graphic editing will let you solve the problem easily. By viewing the notes graphically, you can see which note is longer (literally longer on the screen) and adjust its length accordingly. Graphic editing can also make changing the shape of a pitch bend as simple as redrawing the shape of the bend on the screen. Does the bend go too far down? Redraw its shape to decrease the depth right there on the screen.

If you read music, notation editing makes finding wrong notes a simple process. Looking for the note that just doesn't sound right? Look at the screen and find the note that doesn't fit. Editing other things, such as pitch bend or modulation controls, will usually look the same as in the graphic editing mode.

MIDI is data intensive, and the sheer amount of stuff on the screen can get overwhelming very quickly. Most software sequencers let you filter, or hide, the display of certain data. This can be great if you're looking for a command such as a program change in an event list: set the filter so that the software only displays program changes. Now, instead of wading through hundreds of events, you can find the one you're looking for instantly. When you're done editing, switch the display back to once again show the entire contents of the track.

Many software packages let you predefine which events will be selected for editing based upon specific criteria (such as pitch, note length, or location) and then perform the function on just those notes. You can use a logical editor to find doubled notes, erase notes of very low velocity, or extract a kick-drum part and route it to another instrument, and much, much more.

Audio

Traditional sequencers have always been limited by their inability to record "real" instruments. The audio functions found on most software sequencers eliminates this problem. Now, much of the editing capability once reserved for the MIDI domain can be applied to audio tracks, as well.

When a sequencer records audio, it creates a new file (called an audio file) which it stores on the computer's hard disk. These files are linked to the sequence file. Audio files can be recorded in a number of formats, sampling rates, and resolutions. The most common is 16-bit, 44kHz, the same resolution and sampling rate found on CDs. As of this writing, higher end systems can record audio at 24-bit resolution and sampling rates of 96kHz. The number of audio tracks you can record depends on the capabilities of your audio card, software, and computer: Multi-track audio requires a fast hard drive and plenty of RAM, although recordings of up to eight tracks can be made on relatively modest systems.

Once recorded, audio tracks can be snipped up into pieces and moved around the arrangement, copied, looped, and muted, just like MIDI data. Some programs also allow you to perform advanced functions, such as **time-stretching** (changing duration without changing pitch), **pitch-shifting** (changing pitch without changing the length of the audio clip), reversing the audio, fade ins and outs, and much more. Many sequencers allow you to use a piece of audio to define the tempo of the arrangement, which makes integrating audio and MIDI much easier. Some even allow you to extract audio data and convert it into MIDI data.

Integrated Systems

One of the most powerful features found in a software sequencer is its ability to integrate and mix audio and MIDI. In many systems, audio tracks can be routed through a software emulation of a mixing console. Here EQ and other real-time effects can be applied to the tracks — just like a real mixer. The effects are called *plug-ins*.

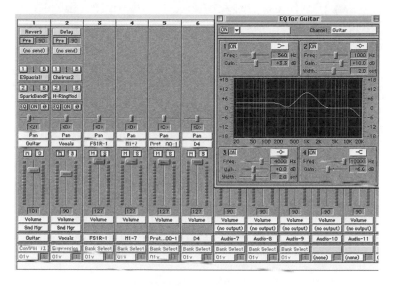

A software-based mixing console

There are two types of real-time plug-ins: hardware based (where the computer controls a dedicated hardware component, usually attached to the sound card), and *native* or software based. Native plug-ins rely on the computer's built-in processor to handle sound. With the increase in processing speed, native plug-ins have become as effective and powerful as many hardware-based effects units.

Even if your computer isn't fast enough to handle real-time native plug-ins, you should be able to apply effects to the audio with file-based plug-ins. These are sometimes referred to as destructive, not because they ruin your recordings, but because they permanently alter the audio file they are applied to.

Automation, Movies, and More

Because sequencers allow you to record many different tracks of audio and MIDI, mixing everything down to a final master can be a daunting task. Fortunately, many sequencers allow you to automate mixes and store them for later recall. In a way, it's just like recording MIDI — you perform the "moves" you want to hear — set volume, pan position, mute status, effects parameters. On playback, the sequencer will replay these moves as you've laid them in. Like other sequencer data, the mix can be edited to perfection.

Computer sequencers also let you import digital video. You can synchronize the video with your music and create a new soundtrack for it. When you start the sequencer, the video will follow along in perfect time.

Many computer sequencers also offer specialized features, such as the ability to communicate directly with an outboard sampler via SCSI; the ability to integrate with patch-editor/librarian software; the ability to load audio directly from CD; built-in audio waveform editors; automatic MIDI processors; and much more.

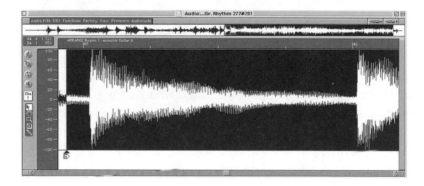

A sequencer's waveform editor lets you edit audio with microscopic precision.

The Outer Limits

Recently, a new category of software has emerged that, though not technically sequencing software, uses sequencing principles to handle music. Some packages deal with audio loops exclusively but treat them in much the same way that traditional sequencers treat MIDI. This allows you to change the length, pitch, timing, and in some cases, the feel of a piece of audio as the track plays back.

Another new category is the software emulation of old analog drum machines and arpeggiators. These programs run resident inside a computer, producing sound through software rather than any electronic circuits of their own. They can be used as stand-alone devices or be synched to another software or hardware sequencer via MIDI.

Weighing the Evidence

There are advantages and disadvantages to software sequencers as compared to hardware units. Your particular needs will determine which is appropriate for you. Performers should be aware that desktop computers usually require more time to set up and pack up than hardware sequencers. They also take up more space and generally are less roadworthy. Fortunately, laptops have become more affordable and have begun to rival their desktop cousins in power. Another alternative is to use a computer to create and edit sequences at home or in the studio, then record them into a hardware unit for use on the road.

7.
MAKING *CONNECTIONS*

YOU HAVE BEEN VERY PATIENT SO FAR. If you are the typical MIDI user, the first thing you want to do with a new piece of equipment is use it. Rare is the person who reads the manual and only then plugs the new toy in. Well, you've waited long enough. Let's rip open some boxes and hook the gizmos up.

There are a number of different configurations that you can employ when setting up a MIDI system that includes a sequencer. Your setup will depend upon the equipment you have. There are, however, some general guidelines to follow:

- MIDI OUT ports are connected to MIDI IN ports. MIDI OUT transmits MIDI information; MIDI IN receives it. (By the way, connections are made with MIDI cables, which have identical connectors on both ends.)

- MIDI THRU ports are connected to MIDI IN ports. MIDI THRU passes along the information coming into the MIDI IN port. You'll see the usefulness of this in the discussion of various system configurations.

Simple Systems

The simplest system is a keyboard with a built-in sequencer and no external modules. It is self-contained and requires no external MIDI connections at all. Plug in the keyboard and go. These systems can be small portable or home keyboards, or full-blown professional "workstations."

Next, you could hook up an external module to your single keyboard. This module could be a drum machine, a tone module, or another keyboard. The keyboard from which you record is called the **master**; the external module is called the **slave**. To set up this system:

- Connect the MIDI OUT of the master to the MIDI IN of the slave.

- Next, connect the MIDI OUT of the slave to the MIDI IN of the master.

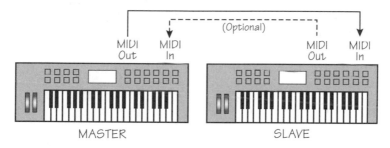

Master keyboard with one slave

This second of these connections is optional. If you decide to make only the single connection, note that the slave cannot talk back to the master keyboard. There is no data line going from the slave to the master. This usually isn't a problem, unless you wish to record into the sequencer from the slave. You may wish to do this if the slave is, for example, a drum machine.

Two-way connection for
recording from the slave

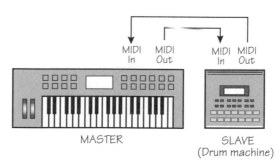

More Slaves!

You can complicate things a little bit more by adding another slave to your system. But where do you connect it? Don't panic! This is where the power of the MIDI THRU port comes into play. Remember that the information coming into a module gets passed on to its MIDI THRU port. The information passes THRU the instrument unchanged (hence the name). To add another slave to your system:

- Connect the MIDI OUT of the master keyboard to the MIDI IN of the first slave.

- Connect the MIDI THRU of the first slave to the MIDI IN of the second slave. The information going to the first unit will go into it, as well as pass through the MIDI THRU port to the second unit.

- If more modules are involved, continue to daisy-chain them together using the MIDI THRU ports.

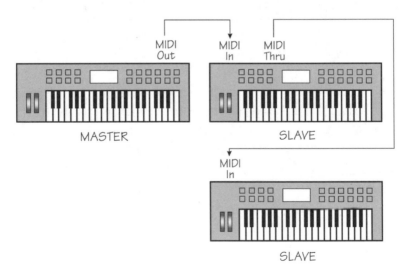

Daisy-chaining multiple slaves

Internalizing the Externals

What happens when you have an external sequencer and not a built-in model in your keyboard? The connections will be similar to those of the master keyboard/slave module setup.

To hook up a system with a hardware sequencer and a single keyboard:

- Connect the MIDI OUT of the sequencer to the MIDI IN of the keyboard.

- Connect the MIDI OUT of the keyboard to the MIDI IN of the sequencer.

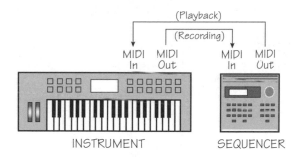

Connections for one instrument and an external sequencer

This system differs slightly from the master keyboard/slave module setup. Both connections are necessary in this case. MIDI data must be able to go from the sequencer to the keyboard. Without this connection, the keyboard will receive no data from the sequencer and will make no sound when you try to play the sequence. Likewise, data must be able to go from the keyboard into the sequencer. Without this connection, no data will get into the sequencer and therefore nothing will be recorded by it.

Over, Under, Out, and Thru

If you will be using several modules, it may be worthwhile to look into a MIDI THRU box, MIDI patchbay, or sequencer with several MIDI OUT ports. A THRU box provides multiple MIDI

OUT ports from a single MIDI IN port. Daisy-chaining can result in some instruments down the chain responding erratically. A THRU box, or multiple MIDI OUT ports, should solve this problem.

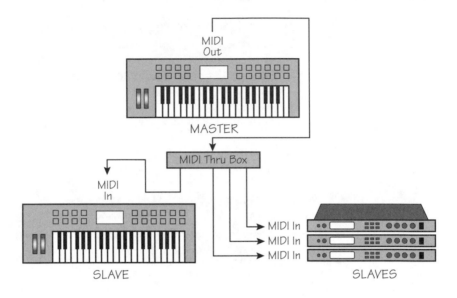

A MIDI THRU box in action

To use a MIDI THRU box:

- Connect the MIDI OUT of the sequencer to the MIDI IN of the THRU box.

- Connect the MIDI OUT of the master keyboard to the MIDI IN of the sequencer.

- Connect a MIDI OUT from the THRU box to the MIDI IN of the master keyboard.

- Connect all the slave instruments to the THRU box by connecting the MIDI OUTs from the box to the MIDI INs of the slaves.

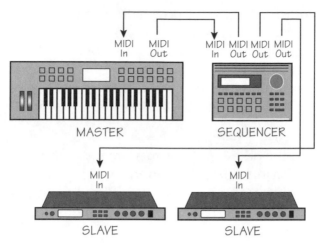

MIDI In MIDI Out   MIDI In MIDI Out MIDI Out MIDI Out

MASTER   SEQUENCER

MIDI In   MIDI In

SLAVE   SLAVE

Using a sequencer with multiple MIDI OUTs

To hook up a sequencer with multiple MIDI OUT ports:

- Connect the MIDI IN of the sequencer to the MIDI OUT of the master keyboard.

- Connect a MIDI OUT from the sequencer to the MIDI IN of the master keyboard.

- Connect all the slave instruments to the sequencer by plugging the MIDI OUTs from the sequencer into the MIDI INs of the slaves.

So what's the big deal about using multiple MIDI outs, other than to impress your friends with big words? Understand that MIDI is a *serial* language. That is a fancy way of saying that MIDI messages get sent down the cable one at a time. A sequencer, to play a single note, has to tell the keyboard, "I have a note on. It's note number 55. The key went down this fast." Each of these messages gets sent down the MIDI cable one at a time. But what does this have to do with multiple outs?

Ever been in a traffic jam? Too many cars in too little space and what happens, besides lots of car horns and colorful language? The traffic stops. The same thing can happen in a MIDI cable.

Too much information going down the cable at one time can cause a jam just like on the freeway. By spreading out the "traffic" of information over more than one MIDI cable, you can avoid the congestion and keep the traffic flowing. If you are using a large number of MIDI instruments, use of a sequencer with multiple MIDI OUT ports can keep the data flowing down the cables.

In some cases, the additional outputs are independent from one another. This means that additional MIDI channels will be available — up to 16 for each port. This used to be reserved for computer interfaces, but has become more common on higher end hardware sequencers as well.

Computer Connections

One of the primary advantages of a computer-based sequencer is its ability to interact with a multi-cable MIDI interface. The hardware sequencers we looked at in Chapter 5 were limited to none or two MIDI out ports that were capable of transmitting on a maximum of 32 different MIDI channels. Most hardware sequencers don't even offer this much — they're limited to 16 channels.

2 x 2 interface

A 2 x 2 MIDI interface (above) can process up to 32 channels of MIDI data; an 8 x 8 interface (below) up to 128 channels. Many of these multiport interfaces can be stacked into larger systems.

8 x 8 interfaces stacked

Whatever type of MIDI interface you choose, you must connect it to your computer in order for it to work. These connections can be made via your computer's serial ports or, increasingly, via USB. If you're using a serial port, your interface may have to share a port with a printer or modem. Some interfaces allow you to connect a printer or modem "in line" so that you can use these devices without having to reconnect them or add serial port expansion, but that's not the case with all of them.

Computers address the interface via software called **drivers**. The method of setting up the interface varies depending on the model, the computer platform, and the sequencing software you are using, but there are some constants across all systems.

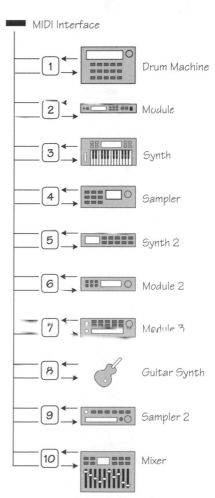

Defining Ports

Before software can play a MIDI device, it has to know where to find it. Most software allows you to pre-configure and name the ports on your MIDI interface for a particular device. Let's say your system consists of a six-port interface connected to a variety of controllers and modules, as shown in the illustration at right.

OMS, or Open Music System, is helper software used by a wide variety of third party programs.

Without helper software, trying to remember which port is connected to what device would be pretty tedious. Instead, we can name each device and say a little about its capabilities. When we're ready to use our sequencer, we can assign tracks to that device by name. We may even be able to store that device's patch information in our sequencer and assign the sounds we want to hear by name, as well.

Whew! What a lot of ground to cover. But don't worry. To hook up a sequencer, just follow the diagrams and you shouldn't get into too much trouble. If you are having trouble, read on, MacDuff.

8.

DON'T *PANIC!*

MIDI SYSTEMS AREN'T MAGIC. The phase of the moon won't affect them, nor will any incense or incantations. The reason a problem occurs will almost always be something logical that was overlooked. If you're like me, your forehead may get a little damaged from the, "Why didn't I notice that before?" syndrome.

Being of Sound Mind

Listed below, and on the following page, are variations on the most basic problem: failure to produce a sound. The possible causes are given, along with solutions to correct them. For a comprehensive discussion of MIDI troubleshooting, see *What's MIDI?* by Jon F. Eiche (Hal Leonard Corporation, 2000).

If your instruments are making no sound at all:

- Are they connected to an audio amplifier and are all volume knobs turned up? (You, there in the back, quit snickering! This may sound funny, but it's happened to all of us at some point in time.)

If one of the slave units is making no sound:

- Are the MIDI connections correct? Is there a bad cable? Double-check the connections and connect a cable you know is good.

- Are all components of the system turned on? If a unit isn't on, it can't pass MIDI data to the THRU port, which will result in inactive instruments in a daisy chain.

- Are the MIDI channel assignments correct? Double-check them.

- Check to see if the sequencer's *soft thru* function (also called *echo back*, or *patch thru*) is on. This feature turns the MIDI OUT port into both an OUT and a THRU. It is used to allow you to hear the slaves when recording from the master.

- Make sure that all control messages (such as MIDI volume) and patch change messages have been reset to the proper value.

Most of the time, a problem is something simple that has been overlooked. Don't panic, breathe deeply, and dive in calmly. Remember, there's nothing magic about MIDI.

9.
TIPS, TRICKS AND TIMESAVERS

SO YOU BOUGHT A SEQUENCER. Now what do you do? This chapter will offer some practical tips for dealing with a MIDI sequencing system and discuss some advanced features that your sequencer may have.

Thanks for the Memory

One of the most important considerations when working with a hardware sequencer is wise use of the available memory. Many newer models offer the capacity for tens- and even hundreds-of-thousands of notes, but on some models (especially older ones) you may find yourself running out of memory more quickly than you expect. When you run out of memory, you run out of room to record more notes. But how can this be? Did you misjudge the number of notes? Is the unit defective? No, you just need to take a little closer look at the MIDI language.

Remember that for a part to be played via MIDI, there is more information than just the notes being recorded. Along with keeping track of which keys are pressed and how fast, the sequencer records aftertouch (how much pressure is put on the key after it is pressed), the pressing and releasing of the sustain pedal, any movement of the mod wheel or pitch bender, and other such information. (This assumes that the instrument is transmitting this information in the first place; not all instruments transmit all of these kinds of MIDI data.) It is all this extra traffic that eats up available memory. When you read that the sequencer can record 20,000 notes, what it really means is 20,000 *events*. If no other data were recorded, the unit could record 20,000 notes. But all this other "stuff" counts as events as well. Where does that leave you? Fear not and tarry awhile longer.

Memory Conservation Conversation

Sequencers often give you the option of filtering out, or **thinning**, certain types of data. Using this option will decrease the amount of information with which the sequencer must deal with and will free up valuable memory. There is no point in recording data that isn't necessary. Aftertouch, usually used to add vibrato, isn't needed on a pipe organ track. Save that memory and filter that data out. Pitch bend messages can often be thinned (some of them removed) with no audible difference in the sound. Not only does this free up space in memory, it will also cut down on the dreaded clog of MIDI data that may happen in a large sequencing system.

Looping, pattern-based sequencing, and the sequences-linked-as-a-song approach, discussed in Chapter 4, also conserve memory by allowing you to record something once (and consequently store it in memory only once), but have it play back several times as needed.

Minding (and Mending) Your Patch Changes

The sequencer can also record patch changes for you. Rather than setting each instrument to the desired sound by hand, have the sequencer do it for you. Be aware that not all instruments process patch changes in the same amount of time. Depending on the model of instrument you are using, the time it takes to process and execute a patch change can be quite long — up to a second on some instruments. While a second isn't usually considered a long time, it is an eternity while you are waiting for a new sound to come up on your keyboard or module. The instrument can't play any notes during this time. The musical flow of a piece can be thoroughly destroyed by a thoughtless patch change. Plan ahead and allow enough time for the instrument to process the patch change command. Wait for a spot where the particular instrument isn't playing before inserting a patch change command. With a heavy flow of MIDI data, patch changes need to be thoughtfully planned.

Multiple Personalities

To give you more for your dollar, many manufacturers are creating instruments that are **multitimbral**. This is a fancy way of saying that the instrument will play more than one sound at a time. These different sounds can be set to different MIDI channels, an ideal situation for sequencing. You don't need a separate keyboard or module for each sound you want. By setting up these wonder boxes, you can get sounds such as strings, piano, bass, and even drums out of one instrument. Simply set each part to the appropriate sound you want and go.

Unfortunately, every silver cloud has a dark lining. (Well, maybe not every one.) One of the most important things to keep track of when using a multitimbral unit (or any MIDI instrument, for that matter) is the number of notes available. An instrument cannot produce more notes than it was designed to. If the keyboard was built to play 16 notes and the piano part needs 14 of those notes in a particular spot, only 2 notes will be left for whatever other parts may be playing there. The polyphony (number of notes) is divided among the different parts. It's annoying to listen to an otherwise wonderful sequence, only to find notes missing in it because it is trying to play too many at the same time.

Chasing Rainbows

One of the most baffling phenomena in the wonderful world of MIDI has a number of symptoms. What in the world could cause these horrific results:

- You stop somewhere in the middle of a sequence, fast-forward several measures, and upon starting again your keyboard is suddenly out of tune.

- You start somewhere in the middle of the sequence only to find that your well-planned and up to now flawless patch changes are seemingly worthless because the parts are being played by the wrong sounds.

The cause of both these problems is quite simple and with some sequencers quite easy to correct.

Suppose you have recorded a sequence and have placed patch change commands at the beginning. These patch changes are flawless, until you start in the middle of the sequence. By starting in the middle of the sequence, after the patch changes, these commands are never sent to the instrument. The instrument can't change patches if the sequencer doesn't tell it to do so. That is, without a feature called *event chasing*.

Event chasing is a handy little option that will scan data in the sequence prior to the start point. Scanning automatically for certain MIDI commands, it will tell the sequencer to send commands to the instruments prior to starting playback. For instance, with event chasing on and set to scan for patch changes, the sequencer will look at the sequence, find the closest prior patch change command in each part and send it automatically. This feature can scan for patch changes, pitch bend commands (the cause of the keyboard being out of tune), and many other MIDI commands and controllers. It can save a lot of head scratching and hours of frustration spent trying to solve a problem with a simple cause.

A Different Drummer

Another possible source of confusion can result from synching together a sequencer and a drum machine (or two sequencers). Some quite interesting, though most often not musical, things can result from drum machines that are not synchronized correctly to the sequencer. Here is our scenario: You have programmed your drum machine to play the drum part for your latest sequence. Trying to play everything back doesn't quite work, though. The drums are playing one tempo while the sequencer plays another. What is the matter?

The sequencer, when the Play button is pushed, sends out a command that says in plain English, "Start." That triggers the Play button for units such as drum machines. Where trouble can creep in, though, is in the synchronization of the drum machine to the sequencer. If the drum machine isn't being told by the sequencer how fast to go, it will go on its merry way, playing at its own tempo. The drum machine's "clock" needs to be set to receive the timing information from the sequencer. Its clock needs to be set to "MIDI," or "External." With the drum machine in this mode, it will receive the commands from the sequencer to keep it playing at the same tempo.

Pointing the Way

In addition to synchronization, there is another potential snare when using a drum machine. If you want to start a sequence somewhere in the middle, how will the drum machine know where to start? It gets the "Start" command from the sequencer all right, but remember, you aren't starting at the beginning. The drum machine needs to be told where the sequencer is starting in order for it to start in the right place as well. The **MIDI Song Position Pointer** command does just that. This is a command that is sent out saying, "I'm at measure 27." A Song Position Pointer message will tell the drum machine to start at the correct spot, while the MIDI clock (synchronization) commands will keep the drum machine and sequencer in perfect time.

Sequencers can also synchronize to audio and videotape decks using **MIDI Time Code (MTC)** — a MIDI representation of SMPTE time code, which follows hours:minutes:seconds:frames. With MTC and **MIDI Machine Control (MMC),** your sequencer can control most of the features on your tape decks.

MIDI can also be used to control audio mixers and effects parameters in real time. Messages addressing these devices can be recorded and edited by your sequencer, just like other MIDI data.

The subject of sequencing is a vast one. Each sequencer has unique features and approaches. But with the basic knowledge you now have, you can ask intelligent questions and read the manuals with greater comprehension.

OUT-TRODUCTION

SEQUENCING TRULY IS A BIG TOPIC. Only the surface has been scratched here. A sequencer is a musical instrument, and as such, it takes practice and patience to master. With the basic knowledge you've gained, you know enough to ask the right questions. No sequencer is the same as another. All the different brands and models have different features and advantages. The choice will be up to you.

Take the time to learn about, and master, your sequencer. It can be a valuable tool in music making. It is a tool that can make your music more exciting and alive. But, just like many other things, you will only get out of it what you put into it. A sequencer can help create music more quickly and easily. But just because it's faster and easier doesn't mean it's good. A sequencer won't make the music good or bad. That part is still up to you.

There isn't any magic to it, just a little time and patience. But the results of some good hard work can be very satisfying. Enjoy!

GLOSSARY

Audio File: A digital recording that has been saved to hard disk. Common formats include .wav, AIFF, and .sd2.

Drum Machine: A device that can be used to create and play back electronic drum sounds created by *samples* stored inside the machine.

General MIDI: A standard that specifies sound and controller assignments, voice allocation, and other aspects of the operation of compatible MIDI instruments.

Master: A MIDI device that controls others.

MIDI: Musical Instrument Digital Interface, a serial connection that allows compatible instruments to communicate with one another.

MIDI Clocks and Song Position Pointer: MIDI timing messages that allow MIDI devices to synchronize based on tempo and song position.

MIDI Machine Control: System Exclusive messages that can be used to remotely control tape and hard disk recorders.

MIDI Time Code: A combination of MIDI timing and system exclusive (sysex) messages that allows MIDI devices to synchronize to absolute time.

Monophonic: A monophonic instrument can play one note or voice at a time. Many polyphonic instruments can have one or more voices play back in "mono" mode.

Multitimbral: A multitimbral instrument can play more than one voice (or sound) independently. Each sound is played back on its own MIDI channel. Multitimbral instruments are especially useful with sequencers.

Polyphonic/Polyphony: A polyphonic instrument can play more than one voice at a time. Polyphony refers to the number of voices available: for example, a synth with 16-voice polyphony can play 16 voices at one time.

Sampler: An electronic instrument that uses digital recordings to create life-like sounds.

Sequencer: A device for the recording, editing, and playback of MIDI information.

Slave: A MIDI device that is controlled by others.

Standard MIDI File: A sequence file format that can be exchanged between devices of different types and manufacturers.

Synthesizer: An instrument that generates sound by the creation and manipulation of artificial waveforms.

INDEX

ABOUT THE AUTHORS

GREG R. STARR is an arranger, writer, and editor. Hailing from the Pacific Northwest, he has taught math and electronic music courses at a junior college. He has also been known to moonlight as a lounge lizard.

In addition to working with pen (or computer) and paper, he applies his knowledge of sequencing and synthesis to produce recordings.

Greg is married, but he does not own a dog named Fido.

EMILE MENASCHÉ is a writer, editor, composer, and producer living in the New York metro area.

What's A...?

Your Answers to Understanding New Music Technology

These completely updated and revised editions present the technology behind modern music-making in a fun, approachable format. With user-friendly text and diagrams, this series is a must-have for all aspiring musicians in the digital age!

WHAT'S A SAMPLER? – REVISED

A Basic Guide to the World of Digital Sampling
by Freff

This quick study removes the intimidation factor from digital sampling by clearly and concisely explaining the technology that makes it tick. Within the space of 56 pages, readers are taken from "The Basics of Sound" to "Truncating and Looping." Readers learn not only how the technology works, but how to create and utilize their own samples.

_____00330526 (56 pages) $6.95

WHAT'S A SEQUENCER? – REVISED

A Basic Guide to Their Features and Use
by Greg R. Starr

No, you don't need a degree in computer science to operate your sequencer, and this basic guide shows you why. *What's a Sequencer?* is valuable to experienced and new users alike. Those already trained will learn how to get more out of their systems, while the uninitiated will see that sequencers can be invaluable – and easily understood – tools of the trade.

_____00330529 (64 pages) $6.95

WHAT'S A SYNTHESIZER? – REVISED

Simple Answers to Common Questions
by Jon F. Eiche

The synthesizer changed the way we make music long ago, and new developments in synth technology emerge every year. But all of those buttons and blinking lights can scare off musicians who want access to the magic inside. Never fear! The whats, hows, and whys are all answered in this guide, which makes the operation and understanding of synths both simple and approachable.

_____00330528 (64 pages) $6.95

WHAT'S MIDI? – REVISED

Making Musical Instruments Work Together
by Jon F. Eiche

At last, a MIDI primer for the rest of us! Understanding the language that allows musical instruments to interface digitally is crucial for today's players, and this handy guide is the perfect place to start. *What's MIDI?* lays out all the essentials without bogging down newcomers in techno-talk.

_____00330527 (56 pages) $6.95

Prices, contents, & availability subject to change without notice.

FOR MORE INFORMATION, SEE YOUR LOCAL MUSIC DEALER, OR WRITE TO:

HAL•LEONARD®
CORPORATION
7777 W. BLUEMOUND RD. P.O. BOX 13819 MILWAUKEE, WI 53213

Visit Hal Leonard Online at
www.halleonard.com